SIMPLE
Gatherings

MELISSA MICHAELS

HARVEST HOUSE PUBLISHERS
EUGENE, OREGON

Scripture quotations are taken from the *Holy Bible*, New Living Translation, copyright
© 1996, 2004, 2007, 2013 by Tyndale House Foundation. Used by permission of Tyndale
House Publishers, Inc., Carol Stream, Illinois 60188. All rights reserved.

Cover by Nicole Dougherty
Cover Image © Vector, Eisfrei / Shutterstock
Interior Design by Faceout Studio, Paul Nielsen

Published in association with William K. Jensen Literary Agency, 119 Bampton Court, Eugene,
Oregon 97404.

SIMPLE GATHERINGS
Copyright © 2017 by Melissa Michaels
Published by Harvest House Publishers
Eugene, Oregon 97402
www.harvesthousepublishers.com

ISBN 978-0-7369-6313-8 (pbk.)
ISBN 978-0-7369-6314-5 (eBook)

Library of Congress Cataloging-in-Publication Data

Names: Michaels, Melissa, author.
Title: Simple gatherings / Melissa Michaels.
Description: Eugene, Oregon : Harvest House Publishers, [2017]
Identifiers: LCCN 2017003032 (print) | LCCN 2017004592 (ebook) | ISBN
    9780736963138 (pbk.) | ISBN 9780736963145 (ebook)
Subjects: LCSH: Entertaining.
Classification: LCC GV1471 .M635 2017 (print) | LCC GV1471 (ebook) | DDC
    793.2--dc23
LC record available at https://lccn.loc.gov/2017003032

Printed in China

17 18 19 20 21 22 23 24 25 / RDS – FO / 10 9 8 7 6 5 4 3 2 1

*Simple gatherings create opportunities to
draw close—to gather around a table, let our
guards down, share our common imperfections,
celebrate our stories, forge lasting friendships,
and connect on a heart level.*

MELISSA MICHAELS

Contents

LET'S GATHER INDOORS {A WEEKEND BRUNCH} 66

THE CONVERSATION 75

LET'S GATHER WITH KIDS {AN ICE-CREAM SUNDAE PARTY} 88

THE SPECIAL TOUCHES 101

LET'S GATHER TO CELEBRATE {AN AFTERNOON DESSERT} 112

AN INVITATION

to Gather

I'm convinced I have a house-shaped heart. Creating a welcoming atmosphere in a home (park, backyard, or church) for family and friends is my love language. Does that mean I have a perfectly kept house and I'm a perfect hostess? Far from it. Come on over, and you'll see plenty of imperfections and likely a bit of pandemonium. That's why long ago I determined that I had to be a laid-back hostess or I'd never invite anyone over! I've found ways to work around my weaknesses and have a lot of fun with my strengths.

My joy in gathering people together doesn't come from a desire to host an over-the-top, Pinterest-worthy party. My heart is stirred to create an intentional and meaningful experience to connect people to one another. As a home decor blogger, church planter's wife, and mom of three, my house-shaped heart has come in handy. Preparing an inviting place for others is how my heart and soul come alive.

In spite of my passion for creating a comfortable home, I don't have it all together. In fact, I'm missing two key ingredients most people associate with a born hostess: I'm not drawn to cooking, and—dun-dun-dun—I'm not an extrovert. Cooking just isn't my thing. And although I enjoy conversation (as my husband can attest to), if the environment is awkward or draining, I want to quietly slip away or tiptoe upstairs and leave the partying to the extroverts.

Maybe you also feel as if you're missing a few ingredients that would help you host with greater ease. If you have the cooking part down, maybe you worry about your small house or your lack of party-planning skills. Perhaps you think your budget or creativity is too limited or that the ages of your kids, your loud dogs, or your wavering sanity might tip you over the edge if you invite people over. I get that.

I've had all of those concerns at one point or another in my life, and *often all at once*. There are endless worries, excuses, or challenges that could prevent us from accepting the title of Hostess with the Mostess. But if we think genuine hospitality means doing it

all perfectly, we've missed the point. *Not being perfectly prepared or equipped is exactly what brings people together in an authentic way.* The purpose of hospitality is to make people feel comfortable, not to impress them with our amazing talent or skill!

In the school of simple gatherings, there is just one rule: Don't worry about rules. Simple gatherings should be as stress-free as possible, so don't fret about the right or wrong way to gather or express your style, and don't fear what might be expected of you as a hostess. (Who makes up those party-hosting rules anyway?)

—— ✦ ✦ ✦ ——

WHAT GUESTS REMEMBER

When you stay focused on your guests, you can take care of the small details in a way that makes them feel celebrated and comfortable in your home. Over the years I've noticed four standout things guests remember. They are the aspects of a visit you will hear guests mention with appreciation to others or to you long after the gathering is over. They are:

THE ATMOSPHERE

THE FEAST

THE CONVERSATION

THE SPECIAL TOUCHES

I will show you how, with some simple preparations, you can pull off warm and gracious celebrations in tune with who you really are. As you go through this book, incorporate the ideas that inspire you or give you greater confidence to gather others in your home. Let's start planning a few simple gatherings that will help you connect and celebrate with a minimum amount of stress and a maximum amount of joy.

Serve one another in love.

GALATIANS 5:13

Get Ready
TO GATHER

Get Ready
TO GATHER

Have you ever visited a home where you felt welcome the moment you crossed the threshold? While the wonderful people greeting you at the door are partially responsible for that, the interior spaces can also reflect warmth and extend a pleasant invitation to come on in.

How do you go about creating an inviting home? The first step is to identify what makes *you* feel at home. If you are comfortable and happy there, it's likely your guests will be too. Your personal spaces should well-loved and authentic reflections of who you are and what you love. When we can observe and celebrate the beauty *and* the imperfections, we're able to open up our doors to the life-changing experience of community.

Let's look at some simple ways to help any home reflect the heart of welcome. Pare away the clutter, do a bit of rearranging, add in some special touches, and before you know it, you'll be racking your brain for yet another reason to have people over. I promise.

When we can observe and celebrate the beauty and the imperfections, we're able to open up our doors to the life-changing experience of community.

1 | DISCOVER REASONS TO GATHER

Each and every day, something is worth celebrating! While big occasions—birthdays, holidays, graduations, anniversaries, engagements, bridal or baby showers—always call for a party, small occasions can call for a party too. Pick a reason to gather from this list, or let it inspire you to come up with some of your own.

SEASONAL

+ Welcome spring (or summer... or autumn...or winter)

+ Mother's Day and Father's Day

+ Garden party (feature fresh food from your garden)

+ Summer pool party

+ Backyard campfire/s'mores/ storytelling

+ Back-to-school

+ Halloween party/trick-or-treating alternative

+ Snow day celebration

+ Christmas lights run or walk (followed by hot cocoa)

+ Cookie decorating (Christmas or Valentine's Day)

CELEBRATIONS AND MILESTONES

+ Birthdays

+ Graduations

+ Engagement or anniversary

+ Bridal or baby showers

+ Congrats on your new job/new home/promotion

+ Going-away party

+ Housewarming/ welcome new neighbors

JUST BECAUSE

+ Appetizer mixer

+ Official National Day of... (example: National Chocolate Day)

+ Movie night or concert on the lawn

+ Afternoon tea

+ Girls' night in

+ Book or movie discussion group

+ Prayer group/Bible study

+ Craft or scrapbooking groups

+ Recipe or cookie swap

+ Family game night

+ Coffee break (because coffee with cookies and conversation is hard to beat!)

2

CELEBRATE YOUR HOSTING STYLE

You can help yourself "be you" when you first identify your style and preferences for hosting and then plan, prep, and put on gatherings in ways that support your style. Consider how each of the four different styles resonates with you. You might be a hybrid hostess who is a Perfectionist during the planning stage and then transforms into an Easy Breezy when the doorbell rings! Whichever rings true for you, my hope is that you'll realize you have what it takes to put together and enjoy a simple gathering (or two or three or...).

PERFECTIONIST

Your attention to detail inspires you to dream up the perfect event. You appreciate the encouragement to sometimes host more laid-back and impromptu get-togethers. Refining your expectations can be key. A what-not-to-do list may be more helpful to you than a to-do list.

EASY BREEZY

You're a carefree, laid-back hostess who is most likely to throw casual, impromptu gatherings. When preparation is necessary, you prefer a simple list of planning tips. Basic party to-do lists can be your best friend because they won't squelch your free-spirited style, and they can prepare you to take your gatherings to a new festive level without added stress.

NERVOUS NESTER

You have a heart for welcoming others to your home, but you end up not committing to hosting because you're paralyzed by what-if worries. Simple gatherings will help you overcome your concerns and allow the guests to be in the spotlight so you can communicate your gracious style on the day of the party.

SOCIAL BUTTERFLY

With a vibrant and social personality, your presence adds to the energy and sets a lively mood for any event. Hosting simple gatherings will allow you to be a part of the festivities and do what you do best—mingling and getting to know people. You want ideas that set the stage for a special but easy-to-manage gathering where you're free to talk, socialize, and savor the experience alongside your guests.

3 | PLAN THE DETAILS: A TO-DO LIST

What's the best way to make sure all the elements of your simple gathering are perfectly pulled together and you have all the necessities you need for a successful, stress-free time? Create a to-do list! Checking off boxes or crossing out chores is super satisfying, and it guarantees you haven't forgotten anything (or anyone!).

— ✦ ✦ ✦ —

HAVE YOU...

☐ Chosen a party theme or decided on an occasion to celebrate?

☐ Written the guest list (and taken a second look to make sure everyone's on it)?

☐ Sent invitations (by email, online invite, or the old-fashioned way—snail mail)?

☐ Considered what is free or low cost in the way of decor, games, and centerpieces? (Hint: Use what you have and shop your home first!)

☐ Thought up enjoyable traditions and rituals you can repeat year after year (or recalled old favorites you've done in the past)?

☐ Planned the menu, taking into consideration any dietary restrictions of your guests?

☐ Made your shopping list (food, drinks, decorations, thanks-for-coming gifts)?

☐ Settled on some entertaining ideas and creative choices for giving your gathering the ideal atmosphere?

☐ Figured out which special touches you'll put into place for a truly memorable simple gathering?

guest list

- Tim + Jenny
- Jake + Kalie
- Emily
- Maci + Nath
- Erik + Anth
- Christina +
- Alexa
- Luke, Ja
- Breegan
- Erin

SHOPPING LIST

- cherry tomatoes
- mozzarella balls (marinated)
- Basil
- Skewers
- 2-3 cakes
- Sorbet
- Juice
- Napkins
- votive candles

4 | ENLIST THE HELP OF OTHERS

Many hands make light work...and a relaxed hostess. Consider in advance how guests can help you before and during the party so you won't be the only one responsible to attend to important details.

+ Invite friends to participate in advance setup or cleanup after.

+ Consider asking for help (or hiring help!) for housecleaning prior to the party and childcare the day of.

+ People always ask if they can bring something, so say yes! It helps lessen your stress, and your guests will feel better not coming empty handed.

+ Consider cohosting. Then you can share in the fun of planning together as well as making sure all the details are taken care of.

+ Ask a friend in advance if they want to help you greet people or serve and replenish food dishes. Be sure they don't have a task that requires their attention the entire time. They want to relax and socialize too!

+ Designate a friend or family member to help you be aware of when a guest is leaving so you can say goodbye to them and thank them for coming.

5 | EMBRACE THE "CLEAN ENOUGH" HOUSE

It's quite enjoyable to explore blogs and plan out our gathering decor, but some of us (ahem) just need to get down to business and clean. I love the saying, "You don't want to put lipstick on a donkey." If we try to dress up a messy home with one small, last-minute effort, we probably won't fool anyone or feel great about our house. But it's relatively painless to make and keep our homes gathering-ready.

A pre-gathering goal for me is to strive for "clean enough," which means I hope that no guest will become injured, stick to the floor, or see anything they will wish they could unsee. I might do more, but no promises. With a few regular cleaning steps, your home can easily be made ready for gatherings, even ones that happen on short notice.

Get a jump start. Grab a box and run through your home, tossing in miscellaneous clutter.

Break it down. Focus more intently on one room or space to unclutter per week.

Maintain. Once your spaces are relatively clean, spend a few minutes daily tidying each area. Touch up the bathrooms a bit each week. This way you won't be overwhelmed the day before a gathering. One helpful way to maintain the overall feel of your home is to take the sniff test. We get used to how our house smells and might not notice an unpleasant scent. Here are my best tips for making sure your house smells good to everyone who enters:

+ Use great-smelling cleaning products in the kitchen and bathrooms. (You can also add essential oils, such as tea tree oil or lavender, to DIY natural cleaners.)

+ Empty your fridge of old food and give the shelves a quick scrub.

+ Vacuum carpet and dust furniture—dirt stinks!

+ Take out the trash and clean litter boxes and animal cages.

+ Give your pets a bath.

+ Light a candle when you're home. Ask your family about the scent to be sure it is sniff-test friendly.

Reward. After an area is clean and organized, you can add the little extras—favorite decorations, natural materials, fragrant soaps, fresh flowers—for your particular gathering. You'll feel an immediate sense of reward for your effort!

6 | PREPARE FOR OVERNIGHT GUESTS

Sometimes an event involves overnight guests staying at your home. If guests are spending the night at my home, I want them to feel as comfortable as if they were at a bed-and-breakfast, even though my house is not big or luxurious, and I don't have a private guest wing. While this requires a little more planning and preparation, with a bit of thinking ahead you can keep even this element of your gathering simple and stress-free. Here are a few things to keep in mind:

+ Clean out your guest room so it is neat, tidy, and welcoming. Remove any personal items from view.

+ Make sure beds are made nicely with fresh, clean sheets, a couple of extra pillows, and extra blankets.

+ Open the window a crack so there is fresh air in the room.

+ Add a small plant or fresh, unscented flowers to the nightstand.

+ Arrange a small basket with mints, trail mix, or other simple snacks.

+ Set out a couple of magazines or books your guests might enjoy reading before bed.

+ Provide clean towels in the guest room or bathroom and let your guests know where they are located.

+ Supply your guest bathroom with a variety of toiletries just in case your guests forgot something.

+ Give your visitors ample privacy in the evenings and early mornings.

7 | CONSIDER THESE DAY-BEFORE TASKS

I promise that if you do a few extra things the day before a gathering, you will be so grateful to yourself for that time and effort. It simplifies the gathering, and it will also ease any concerns you may have.

1. Do a final cleaning of your house the day before. Major housecleaning on the day of a party is stressful and interferes with your preparation (and mood!).

2. Dust your tables and floors before you set up your [serving? dining?] table.

3. Think through how many guests you expect, and then plan the seating and backup seating.

4. Set out your serving platters according to your food presentation preferences. Place notes indicating what food goes where to make party setup a breeze. Make sure your appetizers will fit on the plates you have!

5. Set up simple, decorative embellishments for the food and tables, gather pretty spoons and forks for serving, and place food labels with the serving dishes. Place napkins in convenient locations.

6. Are you serving anything that needs to be thawed? Be sure to keep a simple gathering notepad with reminders, or set a timer for anything that requires removal from the freezer or fridge.

7. Set out drink charms, dry erase markers or homemade labels for your guests' drinks. Everyone can then keep track of their own drink, and they won't need to keep reaching for a new glass.

8. Do a pre-party walk-through. Pretend you're a guest coming into your home. Is the setup welcoming? Is there a spot to hang your coat or set down your purse? Is the bathroom clean and stocked with essentials?

8 | REMEMBER THESE DAY-OF HELPS

Ready, set, go! You can't control every detail and happening, but as you take care of these last few preparations, start letting go of expectations so that you'll be ready to embrace each guest and the meaningful, perfectly imperfect gathering that unfolds.

1. Open the windows wide and let fresh air blow through your home the morning of the party. (Be sparing with scented candles that could aggravate guests' allergies.)

2. Be sure special welcoming touches—flowers, signs, welcome and goodbye stations—are in place and set up with everything you need.

3. Start your get-together on a satisfying note. Set a variety of appetizers and drinks on the tables or at the welcome station just prior to your guests' arrival.

4. If you want to protect tables, have coasters or small napkins available for guests to use.

5. Turn your cell phone ringer on high and vibrate in the hours leading up to and at the start of the party in case a guest tries to reach you. If you used a Facebook event to invite guests, check online in case anyone leaves an updated RSVP or is in need of directions.

6. Do a quick review of the house to make sure everything is in place. Have you tidied up sufficiently? Does the front porch need a quick sweep? Are the food and drinks ready to go? Don't look too closely. A general assessment is all you need.

9 | BE YOURSELF

Creative and intentional hospitality can be simple. The key is to let go of the "have tos" so you can express love, kindness, generosity, and friendship. The unique way *you* set the tone for a meaningful gathering is your gift to others. You just have to be brave enough to start somewhere. Every time you host a gathering, you'll learn something new. I've had lots of practice at failing, but that's how I've figured out what I enjoy and what just isn't my thing!

There are thousands of simple ways you can offer and enjoy the gift of hospitality. Be the life of the party or breathe life into a gathering by celebrating in a way that makes you YOU. If you love preparing a home-cooked meal from scratch, do that. If you get giddy over lighting candles and setting the mood with music, *do that*. If you like to clean...well, it's your party, and you can clean if you want to.

Wherever you find joy in hospitality, *that* is your gift to others. Be real and do that well.

THE
Atmosphere

THE
Atmosphere

Guests will remember the event more vividly when all of their senses are engaged in a happy way. Your party doesn't have to be perfect. Ideally, aim for a few basics that set an inviting tone: a welcoming and relaxed hostess (that's your cue), mood lighting, the smell of good food, and the sound of laughter accompanied by background music. A pretty table, tasty offerings, and lively conversation will make the gathering extra special. Rest assured that a fancy house and a catered meal are *not* required to create a warm and friendly experience.

The thing to know about a home's atmosphere is that it exists whether you've tended to it or not. So paying attention to the feel of your setting is important. The goal isn't to create spaces that impress people in the *ooh-ahh* way...it's to create an environment that makes a good impression on a person's heart and mood. Maybe your atmosphere will put people at ease or even inspire their creativity and happiness. It's such a satisfying process to transform a home into a sanctuary. The simple ideas we'll explore will get you started *and* get you excited about the potential of your home to uplift the people you gather.

It's such a satisfying process to transform a home into a sanctuary.

10 | SIMPLIFY THE INVITATIONS

Your first impression will be made before guests even arrive. Creative invitations allow you to express the atmosphere and style of your chosen gathering, so choose what suits your heart and the festivities to come.

Mailed cards. For a more formal gathering, sending cards through the mail may be the easy way to go. In this digital era, taking the time to mail a personal note or card can help make the event feel extra special.

By phone. It seems that instead of making phone calls, we do everything by text these days. A text can be an easy and quick way to put your gathering together. Just be sure to include all the pertinent details! Also, if you are inviting several people who don't know one another, consider sending the text message to each individual guest. Group texts between lots of unknown phone numbers can make people feel as if they don't know anyone else who has been invited.

Facebook event or email. These days anything goes! A Facebook event notification can help create excitement about a gathering. You can share all the pertinent details and generate excitement with pieces of information, such as a yummy food recipe, a glimpse at your decorations, or a hint at some of the fun activities to expect. It also automatically reminds your invited guests about the event.

Make RSVPing easy. Even if you mail a card, give people the option to text their response, or include stamped, addressed response cards. Take the opportunity to ask about food allergies or special needs to make your guests feel at ease!

★ **Simple tip!** Try postcard-style invitations. They can cut down on cost and time stuffing envelopes.

11 | MAKE A GOOD IMPRESSION

A tidy first impression will make guests look forward to their visit! Even if you don't have a spacious front porch, or the entry to your home is a small stoop and a few steps, you can always welcome your guests in style.

1. Give your porch a good sweeping and clear away any clutter.

2. Wipe down door windows, handles (inside and out), and the doorbell.

3. Take away all unsightly objects. Remove any cobwebs, dirt, or leaves.

4. Set out a clean doormat. You can purchase an inexpensive new mat or just wash the one you have.

5. Once you've taken care of the basics, have fun with seasonal decor. Put out something unexpected, creative, and fresh—a simple green wreath tied with a colorful ribbon, some cheerful plants or flowers, or charming accessories such as a lantern, birdcage, or a ceramic garden stool.

12 | WELCOME GUESTS WITH LIGHT

Nothing says "welcome" like light. If your guests are arriving at night, make sure you turn on all the outside lights. Inside, keep overhead lights at a comfortable level. I love using dimmers and adding warm ambience with lamps.

+ Replace burned-out lightbulbs (inside and outside). Stock a few extra bulbs just in case a significant light burns out during your gathering.

+ Wrap white strings of lights (lovely all year) around windows and doorways.

+ Use paper lanterns for indoor and outdoor gatherings.

+ Dim overhead lights for evening parties, and turn on lamps for a warm, festive glow.

+ Place lit candles (or use flameless candles) throughout the house.

+ Decorate areas with glass or metal lanterns and floating candles in vases.

+ Create a path of mason jar luminaries for your front walkway.

13 | DIY: LIGHT THE WAY WITH MASON JAR LUMINARIES

These easy-to-make luminaries are so warm and welcoming. The salt sparkles and resembles snow or sand. You can be creative with your base material by trying acorns, coffee beans, shells, marbles, beads, cranberries, and so forth. You can also change candle colors to coordinate with your event. (Though I recommend only using white votives with Epsom salt. Colored candles will discolor your salt as it melts.)

WHAT YOU'LL NEED

Mason jars of preferred size

Epsom salt
(found in the pharmacy section)

Long-burning candles
(tea lights, votives, pillars, or flameless candles)

Ribbon or twine if desired

Directions:

1. **Scoop** Epsom salt into the jars.

2. **Add** a candle.

3. **Tie** ribbon or twine around the jars.

4. **Light** the candle and display the luminaries along your front walkway, entryway, outdoor paths, or as centerpieces.

14 | CREATE AN INVITING ENTRY

After the front porch, the entry space gives the next first impression of your home. Here are some simple ways to let your entry say, "Come on in!"

Declutter the entry. Clear away personal items (stacks of mail, boots and shoes, purses and backpacks) so guests have an easy time coming and going. Corral smaller items you plan to leave out in baskets or on trays.

Keep it light. Add a lamp or candles to give your entry a warm glow and welcome your guests, especially in the evening.

Make room for guests' belongings. Create an obvious place for guests to hang their coats and bags so they feel right at home right away. If you don't have a coat closet, you can make a creative coat hanger for a wall with just about anything (shutters, an old door, a wooden stepladder...and add hooks). If you want guests to put personal belongings in a bedroom, remember to tidy the room and make the bed before guests arrive!

Consider the cozy factor. Drape a seasonal table runner on an entry table and place a textured rug in the entry to make it warm and welcoming. You can also add a basket of textured blankets and cute scarves and mittens hanging from hooks.

Create a focal point. This could be a striking table, cabinet, or bench. In smaller entryways, a bold and fabulous mirror can grab attention and reflect light around the room. You can also display a collection of photos in frames. Whatever your focal point is, feel free to embellish it further for your gathering (greenery around the mirror, flowers on the table, cloth bunting banner, or a string of twinkle lights by the photos)

15 | ADD A SPLASH OF COLOR

A small bit of color can make a dramatic impression on the look of your home. There are so many simple ways to add vibrancy or boost the mood of a room with color.

+ Place flowers anywhere (don't forget the bathroom).

+ Set out pretty bowls filled with fruit in your kitchen and living room.

+ Put colorful containers and plants by your front door.

+ Choose one seasonal accent color to contrast with white dishes.

+ Mix and match colorful dishes, serving platters, and centerpieces for a festive feel.

+ Add food coloring to water in glass bowls filled with marbles and a floating candle.

+ Use seasonally colored candles throughout your home.

16 | SET THE MOOD WITH MUSIC

Turn on music at a festive volume prior to the gathering to fill a potentially awkward silence as the gathering gets started. Once enough people arrive, turn down the volume just enough to maintain the lively mood and yet allow your guests to converse comfortably. Consider creating a special playlist for your gathering. Think about the atmosphere you want to create, and find music to fit that feeling.

+ Oldies and/or surf music for a summer pool party

+ Instrumental jazz for a garden party

+ Musical soundtracks for family game night

+ A neighborhood band for a block party

+ Favorite pop tunes for a girls'-night-in party

+ Christmas music for a holiday cookie-decorating party

17 | CREATE COZY WITH TEXTURES

A house is most inviting when it appeals to the senses on many levels. When walking through a forest or along a sandy beach, how does the combination of sights, sounds, scents, and surfaces make you feel? The colors and patterns we select make visual statements, but the tactile experience found in layers of texture help a home come alive.

Textures visually draw you in to a space and create complexity to the feel and look. When you play with textures, you can create a calm and inviting space that is also warm and welcoming. When your guests are able to engage their senses, they'll feel comfortable in your home—no matter if it's their first visit or their fiftieth.

+ Begin by quickly clearing the room of distracting accessories, colors, and patterns that don't contribute to the mood you want.

+ Add in a few quick and easy natural elements—such as green plants, stones or shells on a tray, or pinecones in a bowl. You can even move plants out of other rooms into your main entertaining space to freshen the look.

+ Shed light in a dark room with a light-toned quilt or table runner, a creamy porcelain pitcher or vase, or a glass accessory or lamp base.

+ Layer a rug in your main entertaining space for a cozy feel. (Once again, feel free to move a rug from a less-used space.)

+ Have fun playing around with accessories you already have. Remember, opposites attract. Combine smooth with rugged or shiny with dull.

+ For variety, incorporate glass with display dishes, lamps, or bottles. Add sparkle or shine with mirrors and metals.

+ Toss cozy blankets over sofas and chairs, and add a variety of throw pillows in varying textures so guests can relax and feel at home. (Blankets are great if you have guests who tend to run cold!)

+ Try to weave textural elements into your serving table, entry, and even your guest bathroom too.

18 | SOLVE THE SHOE DILEMMA

It's one of the first things that crosses the mind of every party guest: *Should I leave my shoes on or take them off?* If you're hosting the party, should you have shoes on? And does a pile of shoes by the front door imply a "no shoes" rule, or do you need to be more specific?

A few things to consider:

1. Look at your guest list and consider how the people on it might feel about walking around in socks or bare feet (or in shoes, for that matter).

2. If you do choose to go with a no-shoe rule, make it obvious. A hand-lettered sign or a big basket or special space for shoes can help get your message across.

3. Take the weather into account. Is it snowy or muddy outside?

4. During the party, will guests be going indoors and outdoors frequently?

5. What seems right for your entertaining style and the type of party you're having?

19 EXPRESS SINCERE WELCOMES & GOODBYES

Greetings set the tone for the gathering, and goodbyes set the tone for the memories guests will carry with them long after they leave. Here are some helpful prompts:

1. As you prepare your home, consider each guest. Think of something you appreciate about them, and take a moment to remember the details of what's going on in their lives. When the doorbell rings, you'll be more focused on welcoming each person sincerely and less inclined to stress about dust bunnies or a lopsided cake.

2. Greet everyone at the door with a smile and a sincere welcome.

3. Show your guests where to find the powder room, offer them drinks and snacks, and introduce them to someone. My friend Sandy Coughlin shared this great advice on her blog, *Reluctant Entertainer*: "Introducing our friends for who they are, rather than focusing on what they do or their accomplishments, will make that person feel so good about themselves, secure, loved, and valued before and beyond their accomplishments or 'what they do.' Here's a challenge. The next time you're introducing a friend, focus on their characteristics or virtues *first*, and use those words in your introduction."

4. Send guests home with a small treat so they can have something tangible to remember the fun they had. (See tip 21, "Designate a Goodbye Station," for some simple ideas.)

5. At the end of the get-together, send guests off with a heartfelt goodbye and an "I'm so glad you were here!" Let them return home knowing that the gathering would not have been the same without their presence.

20 | SET UP A WELCOME STATION

A welcome station provides an opportunity for someone to locate friends or fill a small plate with goodies as they get to know other guests.

+ Place a table near the front entry to welcome guests with a few simple snacks as they arrive. This invitation gives each guest a place to go right away and a chance to feel comfortable and connected as they enter your home.

+ If possible, locate the table near the hooks or bowl you have set out for people to place their keys, purses, and other odds and ends.

+ Make it festive. This station can be a great spot to bring in color and creativity. For example, margarita glasses can make salsa or dips feel extra celebratory.

+ Hang up a welcome sign or banner or write your own special welcome message on a chalkboard.

+ If you have access to one, create your station using a dresser or buffet unit. Then store and access the supplies and treats you need for the welcome and the goodbye. Easy!

21 | DESIGNATE A GOODBYE STATION

Use whatever table you used for your welcome station to also see your guests off with intention and grace.

+ Once your guests have been greeted, find a moment during the gathering to swap out your "Welcome" items and signs for those of "Farewell."

+ This goodbye station is a visible way to express gratitude to your guests. For extra-special gatherings, offering a take-home gift in a favor bag is the perfect way to end a memorable event. Set the bags out where guests will see them as they leave. Some items they might enjoy include homemade cookies, a fragrant votive candle, or even a notepad in a pretty bag.

+ You can also make a simple "Until Next Time" sign, write a celebratory quote on a chalkboard, or print a quote from your computer to tape into a frame and place near the front door.

+ If people brought food items or other supplies, consider having a "Don't Forget" sign with a few possible items listed: keys, leftovers, your goody bag, your children (heh).

+ Have your signs and goodies prepared in advance so you can arrange them quickly and easily during the event.

LET'S GATHER OUTDOORS
{A BBQ SLIDER BAR}

When we take a party outdoors, we expand our space and our opportunities to gather. Without a lot of planning, a patio or lawn becomes an ideal place for a casual and magical get-together.

This simple gathering features a gourmet burger in a chic, compact size called a *slider*. The build-your-own-slider experience inspires guests to mingle and conversations to spark. Host a small group of people you are comfortable being around. Have everyone bring a side dish to add to your main course, and then give yourself permission to enjoy the afternoon or evening as if you're a guest at your party. Chat, laugh, load up a slider or two, and don't worry about dishes until later. The joy will outweigh the worry.

The Atmosphere

Even though you can't predict the weather, there are factors you *can* control for your next backyard BBQ, campfire, and so forth. Whether you have a small patch of grass or a multilevel deck, a few simple preparations will help you create a friendly atmosphere with ease so that when the mood strikes, you can invite the guests, light the grill, and let the casual setting be the perfect backdrop to a memorable gathering.

— ✦ ✦ ✦ —

5 WAYS TO BE BBQ READY

1. **Spring-clean outdoors.** Plan an afternoon to weed the garden and trim overgrown foliage, take the patio furniture out of storage and hose it off, sweep the deck, and clean the grill.

2. **Store BBQ supplies together.** Keep skewers, fire pit supplies, and your grill set handy. Stack dry firewood near the fire pit, and stash a supply of BBQ briquettes close to the grill. Being organized will help set a relaxed atmosphere.

3. **Set up creative outdoor seating.** Browse garage sales, set your interior chairs out in the yard, and add portable seating using blankets and pillows. You can make inexpensive, rustic outdoor tables using the large wooden spools electrical companies discard.

4. **Plan ahead so you can be spontaneous later.** Keep a small supply of reusable decorations and stock food basics. Don't forget ingredients for s'mores to please guests of all ages.

5. **Consider the weather.** If it's going to be a hot day (or if there is a chance for rain), make sure you have some covered spots for people to stay cool (or dry).

The Feast

Here is a suggested BBQ Slider Bar sample menu that covers the basics for a good BBQ experience. Feel free to swap these ingredients out with some of your family favorites.

MENU

Sliders
(organic, grass-fed beef formed into small patties)

Slider buns or rolls

Grilled vegetable skewers

Coleslaw

S'mores

Lemonade

SPECIAL TOPPERS

Bacon

Guacamole

Onion rings or canned fried onions

Pepperoni slices

Grilled peppers

Gorgonzola, mozzarella, pepper jack, goat, or blue cheese

Pineapple rings

COLESLAW

This coleslaw recipe is one of my go-to salads for summer.

SALAD:

6 cups red and green shredded
  cabbage
1 cup shredded carrot
1/3 cup cilantro, chopped

DRESSING:

1 cup whole milk yogurt
1 cup olive oil
2 tablespoons rice vinegar
1 teaspoon salt

DELICIOUS COLESLAW ADDITIONS:

Raisins
Dried cranberries
Pomegranate seeds
Sunflower seeds or pistachios
Broccoli slaw
Mandarin orange slices (if canned,
  drain liquid first)
French fried onion rings (toss at the
  last minute so they are crunchy)

Mix dressing ingredients together until well blended. Add desired amount of dressing to the slaw mixture and stir well.

The Conversation

Easy conversation flows at outdoor gatherings. The relaxed, inviting atmosphere provides the setting for connections between friends and those who are meeting for the first time. Create opportunities for guests to mingle and interact by arranging food and beverage stations.

Assigning different tables as your stations for slider creation, drinks, and utensils will make it easy on you and on your guests. Right away, people know they can get in line, chat with the person next to them, and even compare their favorite toppings at the slider station or personal drink blends at the beverage table.

BBQ SLIDER STATION

Place toppings on creative serving surfaces (wooden cutting boards, cookie sheets, decorative baskets) for easy access and a pretty presentation. Then make a clear path from the grill to this station so the cook can deliver a platter of fresh, perfectly grilled slider burgers to set down next to the tray of small buns. (Check your favorite bakery for cute slider buns, such as the ones in my photos.) Use bamboo burger picks to hold the sliders together. Guests can create their perfect sliders while chatting over the toppings table. Go-to basics are onions, pickles, tomatoes, sauces, lettuces, and cheddar and Swiss cheese.

BEVERAGE STATION

At the drink station, guests can choose their favorite fruit to embellish a cold glass of lemonade. Set out raspberries, blueberries, strawberries, and blackberries alongside mint leaves, a pitcher of cold lemonade, and cups so guests can mix their own special drink. Don't forget to provide them with a label to identify their cup.

S'MORES STATION

Create a feeling of nostalgia and coziness around your backyard fire pit with a tantalizing s'mores station. Adults and kids alike will love this activity. Scoop up your cutest serving pieces, fill them with classic and surprising ingredients, and pop them on a pleasing tray. Besides the usual standbys—graham crackers (offer standard and cinnamon), decadent chocolate squares, and marshmallows (the jumbo size are extra fun)—add some eye-catching extras. Raspberries, sliced bananas, and shredded coconut appeal to fruit lovers. Spreads such as peanut butter, strawberry jam, and lemon curd sweeten things with a fun twist. You can even get really bold with bacon bits and salted caramel. Yum!

The Special Touches

Your arrangement of the stations combined with simple decor choices create the special touches for this gathering. Here are some functional and fun accessory inspirations:

+ Mix and match serving piece styles to keep the tables casual. Be creative with what you have. Our favorite use-what-you-have platters and containers are wooden cutting boards, baskets, small cookie sheets, and metal buckets lined with parchment paper.

+ Use kraft paper as an inexpensive tablecloth for easy cleanup. It's also the perfect surface to write on. Label food or draw place settings and place cards with a Sharpie and/or allow guests to doodle.

+ Let nature inspire your decor. Turn a patio into a garden oasis with inexpensive plants and colorful pots, pallets, lattices, and planter boxes from flea markets. Add colorful bowls filled with seasonal fruit or simple vases filled with vibrant glass stones or wildflowers.

+ Add your own individual style. Drape outdoor lights around deck rails and hang lanterns with candles for a festive glow. Use a large metal tub as a charming cooler for ice and drinks.

THE

THE
Feast

Guests feel taken care of at a party when they have a favorite drink in hand and a plate of snacks to nibble on. The food doesn't have to be gourmet or homemade to be special and delicious. To make the experience of feasting more enjoyable, think of ways to set up tables with tasty food that is attractively presented. Even chips and dip feel fancy when placed in pretty bowls. After all, one person's hors d'oeuvres are another person's finger food. It's a matter of mood and attitude.

Your table is your canvas. Consider ways to introduce color with fresh foods and interesting serving dishes, and add personal taste using seasonings of the season or flavors of a region. Above all else, always give yourself permission to keep your food and decor simple. The best shared dining experiences aren't about excess— they're about how you *express* your sincere welcome.

Whether you lean toward rustic or elegant, the intentional choices we'll explore for the preparation and presentation of food will make any buffet spread, family-style meal, barbeque, or assortment of appetizers feel like an abundant feast.

The best shared dining experiences aren't about excess—they're about how you express your sincere welcome.

| # STOCK UP

Here are a few of my favorite staples to have handy for impromptu get-togethers. (Note: Before you head to the store, take a few moments to clear out your refrigerator, freezer, and pantry of old food so you have plenty of room when you return.)

+ Dried pasta and tomato sauce (they're easy to store and make a good last-minute meal)

+ Chips and crackers (we stock gourmet varieties so we don't have to pull out the saltines)

+ Dips and salsas in jars

+ Packaged cookies and frozen cookie dough

+ Olives

+ Mixed nuts

+ A variety of cheeses

+ Fancy chocolate bars

+ Frozen appetizers (we love the options at Trader Joe's)

+ Sparkling water, coffee, tea, bottled lemonade

+ Baking mixes (cakes, cookies, brownies)

23 | GIVE YOURSELF A BREAK

If you love to cook and bake, prepare food the day before if possible to cut down on stress from the last-minute mess. If you don't love to cook and bake or just don't have time, find a local source for good party food! In our area, Costco and Trader Joe's always have delicious and attractive food that is perfect for parties. What could you purchase that would make life easier? Do you really want to make homemade salsa or pizza dough? If so, do it. If not, buy it. Or buy it and embellish it.

Here are ten open-and-go party foods (just add pretty serving pieces!):

1. Sliced bread and bruschetta

2. Nuts (almonds, pecans, pistachios, cashews)

3. Assorted crackers and dips (including the old standby, chips and salsa)

4. Hummus and pita slices

5. Frozen appetizers (pastry bites, stuffed mushrooms)

6. Presliced cheeses, cream cheese, or even a simple baked brie

7. Pot stickers or taquitos (depending on your theme)

8. Jars of pepper jelly, mustards, olives

9. Variety of fancy cookies or cupcakes

10. Cakes, pies, or tortes (look in the frozen section, and be sure to allow time to thaw)

24 | TEST RECIPES IN ADVANCE

Don't wait until the day of the gathering to try out your recipes. Test them early so you can think through the ingredients, taste the end results, and estimate the number of servings. If you're feeling stressed, stick with tried-and-true recipes you know are favorites with your family and friends.

+ Focus on keeping the recipes simple. You don't want to be scrambling to find too many ingredients and spending all your time in the kitchen.

+ Enjoy deceptively simple dishes. Smoothie bowls for a brunch look so elegant, yet all you need to do is whip up the smoothie mix and set out the toppings (sliced fruit, honey, granola, peanut butter, nuts and seeds, shredded coconut) in pretty serving dishes.

+ Add a splash of color. Arrange fresh veggies paired with delicious dips.

+ Consider your family's go-to drink recipes. Think hot or cold—spiced cider, creamy cocoa, flavored lemonade.

+ Don't forget your slow cooker. Slow cooker meals practically make themselves.

25 | ADDRESS THE TRAFFIC FLOW

Think through possible bottlenecks if you are going to serve a larger group in a small space. I like to remove chairs to open up traffic flow around the table and then set up chairs in other rooms for extra seating and conversation areas.

+ You can help people move through the line quicker by making your serving table accessible on both sides. (You may need to have two plates of the same dish so you can place one on each side.)

+ Consider multiple stacks of plates, napkins, and utensils at both ends of the serving table.

+ Make sure food on both sides of the table is refilled to prevent awkward reaching across the table.

+ In your conversation areas, check for adequate lighting in each space. Dark areas seem less friendly. Light candles and move lamps around to provide warm and cozy seating arrangements.

26 | GO BUFFET!

For simplicity and flexibility for you and your guests, plan a simple buffet-style event rather than a formal sit-down dinner. A serve-yourself buffet provides guests options to accommodate various dietary needs and restrictions, and it takes away the stress of unexpected meal fails or wondering how many people will show up for dinner. Here are some of my favorite tips for going buffet:

+ Let go of the idea that you have to do it all. It's totally okay to invite guests to a potluck and set the selections out buffet-style. Bonus: Guests with food allergies love potlucks because they know there's at least one dish they can eat!

+ Collect or create reusable serving and decor pieces for the buffet table rather than using cheap, disposable paper products. This will save you money in the long run, create less waste, and look much more festive.

+ Plan ahead to include a few special touches such as a handmade, reusable cloth banner or fresh flowers and plants on the buffet table.

+ Serve your buffet food on a variety of pretty plates, bowls, and cake stands. A variety of plate sizes is fine too. Some people prefer smaller plates, and some people like big ones, so options are welcomed!

+ Provide a convenient but reasonably attractive place for guests to dispose of trash. If you use real dishes for your buffet-style gathering, the amount of trash generated during a party is minimal and can usually fit in just one bag.

27 | SET UP CREATIVE FOOD STATIONS

If you're entertaining a fairly large group, or if you're limited on space, use a buffet-style setup with various fun food stations. When you can combine activity, food, decor, and theme, you know you have a winner! I stack dishes on my table, put silverware in my caddy, and feature a few appetizer-style dishes (or fruit and rolls for brunches) on my dining room table. Then the rest of the food is set up in the kitchen, potluck-style. Sometimes I put desserts in my dining room (to create more of a delicious dessert destination!), salads on my kitchen table, and main dishes on the kitchen counter. Separating the meal into stations helps with the traffic flow and makes it feel more festive and partylike!

Candy Station. Fill muffin papers with jelly beans, use candy as part of the decor (saltwater taffy is great for a beach-theme party), or fill a basket with cute, bagged candy that serves as party favors for the guests.

Cookie Station. Supply frosting, sprinkles, and other decorative embellishments for cookies, along with plastic knives and cute napkins.

Coffee and Pastry Station. Perfect for a brunch gathering.

Grilled Panini Sandwich Station. Guests can customize their own creations.

Mashed Potato Station. Fill cocktail glasses with mashed potatoes and set out various toppings (shredded cheese, sour cream, chives, bacon bits, butter) in decorative bowls.

Make-Your-Own Station. Guests can create their own tacos, pizzas, salads, drinks, and desserts.

Simple tip! Low on counter space? Use an end table, footstool, or small ladder to serve your food. It provides more surface area and adds height to your display.

28 | CREATE A BEVERAGE STATION

One way to add some flair to your party is to start with your drinks! Simple touches, such as sliced cucumbers or lemons with basil and ice in sparkling lemon-lime soda or even water, will transform your beverage options from ordinary to extraordinary.

Here are some memorable beverage station ideas:

Coffee Station. Use a French press, and offer milk, half-and-half, or creamers in popular flavors such as peppermint or vanilla.

Hot Cocoa Station. Try different flavors of cocoa, such as white chocolate or raspberry dark chocolate, and provide marshmallows, whipped cream, sprinkles, cocoa powder in a shaker, and candy canes to make it pretty and festive.

Italian Soda Station. Set out club soda, a variety of flavored syrups (try vanilla and blackberry together!), and a bucket of ice. Add a pitcher of cream for creamosas.

Lemonade Station. Set out raspberries, blueberries, strawberries, blackberries, and mint leaves in little bowls.

Hot Spiced Cider Station. Warm up some apple cider or apple juice and add your favorite spices. Then set out cinnamon sticks, allspice berries, and orange slices.

Don't forget pretty cups or mugs, straws, and maybe even a chalkboard menu of instructions.

Get creative with labels! Not only do labels cut down on the amount of drink glasses you'll need, but the process of choosing drinks and labeling glasses makes the drink station a festive part of the party. Cut the labels out of stiff paper, write each guest's name on a label—or let them write it themselves—and tie them around the glass with string. (Mason jars or glasses with a handle or stem work well for this.)

Simple tip! Try to avoid serving beverages in punch bowls, as they tend to become sticky and messy.

29 | STEEP FRENCH PRESS COFFEE IN SIX EASY STEPS

For coffee lovers (and who isn't?), a French press can make simple gatherings more special. This coffee-preparation method is not convenient for a bigger party, but it's a neat idea when you have just a few guests...say, for brunch.

If you are intimidated by a French press, you don't need to be. Grind the beans (we like Stumptown organic coffee) just before your gathering, and then follow these simple steps for preparing delicious coffee.

1. **Boil** some water.

2. **Scoop** fresh, coarsely ground coffee into the carafe (2 tablespoons coffee grounds per 6 ounces of water).

3. **Add** boiling water and stir.

4. **Steep** water and coffee for 4 to 5 minutes.

5. **Press** down on the plunger filter slowly.

6. **Serve** delicious, rich coffee to your happy guests.

30 | ENJOY SEASONAL FLAVORS

There's nothing like pumpkin pie (or anything pumpkin flavored!) and hot spiced cider for an autumn gathering. Winter brings the taste of peppermint, hazelnuts, and decadent dark chocolate. And the warmth of spring and summer are perfect for featuring fresh berries and barbeque. Here are some favorite flavors and foods for each season's simple gatherings:

SPRING

Fruit tarts

Poppy seed and/
or blueberry muffins

Cucumber-basil lemonade

Pastel-frosted cupcakes

Dainty tea sandwiches

Pink lemonade

Flavored teas

SUMMER

Strawberry or
raspberry lemonade

Basil and tomato or basil and
cucumber sandwiches

Anything on the barbeque

Fruit salad

Flavored popsicles
(try minty watermelon-lime)

Simple salads fresh
from the garden

AUTUMN

Caramel apples

Anything pumpkin

Roasted root veggies
(potatoes, carrots, beets)

Apple pie

Squash with
buttered brown sugar

Chili with cornbread
smothered in honey

Popcorn

WINTER

Cranberry anything
(try spiced cranberry cider)

Peppermint-rimmed
hot chocolate

Eggnog

Christmas cookies

Cinnamon, orange, or clove

Sweet potato fries

Gingerbread

31 | PUT TOGETHER A PRETTY PRESENTATION

Adopting the K.I.S.S. motto (keep it simple, sweetheart) will serve you and your guests well when it comes to the food. You don't need to be a gourmet chef to create a feast that is visually appetizing. Here are some simple tips and tricks to inspire you to serve your party food with flair and a memorable style.

Take items out of their packaging. Crackers and chips always look more appetizing in a bowl, basket, or lined up on a tray. Remove dips from cartons and place in small bowls. Use creative food labels to identify food as necessary.

Serve it on a skewer. Alternating colors and items add interest. Try:

+ Caprese skewers: tomatoes, mozzarella, and basil

+ Sandwich skewers: small bites of meat, cheese, tomato, lettuce, bread

+ Rainbow fruit skewers: strawberries, watermelon, pineapple, grapes, blueberries

+ Salad skewers: lettuce, carrots, cucumbers, crunchy croutons

+ Dessert skewers: bananas, chocolate, pound cake, strawberries—plus a side of chocolate, caramel, or whipped cream for dipping

Cut out fun shapes. They worked in kindergarten, and adults love fun shapes too! Finger sandwiches can be cut into triangles and held together with fancy toothpicks. Some vegetables or fruit can be cut with small cookie cutters (try it with kiwi, cantaloupe, or watermelon!).

Think about color. Incorporate fresh, natural foods in vivid colors and interesting textures. Maybe add a bowl of bright purple beet hummus next to a bowl of chips or a bread platter.

Give basic dishes an extra gourmet touch. Roasted walnuts or almonds can be added to the top of hot dishes or vegetables. Jazz up the top of a dessert with a sprig of mint, crushed candy canes, cinnamon, cocoa, or powdered sugar.

32 | INCLUDE HEALTHY CHOICES

Some of your guests may have dietary restrictions, so it's helpful to check with everyone in advance of the gathering in order to be sensitive to their needs. If in doubt, or if you want to simplify, be prepared with a variety of healthy choices guests can choose from. Here are some ideas to make your gathering delicious and healthy.

+ Fresh salads with dressing options on the side, including a nondairy oil and vinaigrette dressing, make either a great meal or nutritious addition to an entrée.

+ Dairy-free, nut-free, and gluten-free items come in a lot of possibilities. (Make sure they are clearly labeled.)

+ Avocado, hummus, and Greek yogurt for dips will decorate your food area when placed in pretty bowls.

+ Cucumber slices, apples, carrot sticks, or even kale chips are a satisfying alternative for those who cannot have crackers or bread.

+ DIY lettuce wraps allow your guests to create something to please their particular palate. Simply provide butter lettuce and pre-separate the leaves, as well as, a selection of items such as Feta, sliced cucumbers, diced tomatoes, avocado, edamame, lime, and olive oil.

+ Popcorn is a good low-fat alternative for those trying to avoid heavy snacks.

+ Greek yogurt parfaits with separate granola toppings are delicious option at a brunch.

+ Popsicles are a sweet, refreshing treat for those who cannot have dairy or ice cream.

+ Water or sparkling water as a beverage is preference for many. Set out a tray with fun drink garnishes such as slices of cucumbers, strawberries, basil, mint, limes, grapefruit, or berries!

Simple tip! If preparing food for guests with specific dietary concerns is not something you feel confident handling yourself, perhaps you could ask if they could bring a dish that would be safe for them to eat or ask for their advice on how to be prepared to serve them.

LET'S GATHER INDOORS
{A WEEKEND BRUNCH}

Welcoming guests into our home is a great joy and privilege. The more we do this, the more second nature it will be to say, "Come on over this weekend," and mean it. Indoor gatherings can be fancy dinners, or they can be simple, low-stress get-togethers.

One of our favorite simple gatherings is brunch at home. There's something comforting about breaking bread with a couple of friends at a cozy table. And if that bread happens to be a scone...well, that's all the better!

Connect with friends and family over an easy-to-make gourmet quiche, blueberry scones, and other breakfast favorites. Make your table special with eclectic place settings and coffee to share from a pretty French press. We'll take a look at simple elements that bring people together, awaken their senses and appetites, and create a memorable gathering.

The Atmosphere

Pleasant aromas, sounds, sights, and tastes will create a warm ambience that invites friends and family members to settle in for a time of meaningful connection.

— ✦ ✦ ✦ —

6 KEYS TO A STRESS-FREE BRUNCH

1. Choose brunch recipes you have made before, or practice the dishes in advance.

2. Select a music playlist that will add just the right energy without being annoying to guests who have not yet had their morning coffee.

3. Set the table the day before to make sure you have the right serving dishes. Cover the table with a sheet to keep everything clean overnight.

4. Consider brunch items that can be baked the day before and popped into the oven to reheat just before your gathering. Also, the aroma of something delicious warming in the oven will make your guests happy the moment they arrive.

5. Put out a sign to direct guests to a powder room, or let guests know upon arrival where it is so they don't have to ask, wonder, or wander.

6. More is more! Make extra coffee and food. No one will complain about having leftovers.

The Feast

A brunch can be as simple as a nice selection of baked goods, but I like to have a mix of items. This is my sample menu, along with a simple but gourmet quiche recipe. Choose items you know will please your group of guests and that will make preparation and cleanup simple for you.

MENU

Bacon, kale, and
goat cheese quiche

Homemade blueberry scones

Assorted jams/jellies/honey

Yogurt

Granola

Fruit

Orange juice

French press coffee

Cream/sugar

BACON, KALE, AND GOAT CHEESE QUICHE

5 to 6 strips bacon
3 to 4 kale leaves (removed from stem)
2 garlic cloves, minced
1/2 onion, chopped
6 eggs
1 cup whole milk
1/4 teaspoon salt

1/4 teaspoon pepper
4 ounces goat cheese, crumbled
1/3 cup Parmesan cheese, grated
1 piecrust (make your own or save
   time by using a Marie Callender's
   frozen piecrust)

Preheat oven to 375 degrees. Mold a premade or purchased piecrust to fit a 9-inch pie pan. Cut up the bacon into bite-sized pieces and cook them in a skillet over medium heat. Once browned, add the kale, garlic, and onion. Cook about 5 minutes or until the kale becomes wilted. Put the bacon, kale, garlic, and onion in the uncooked piecrust. Whisk together the eggs, milk, salt, and pepper. Pour this mixture over the bacon mixture. Sprinkle goat cheese over the top and then do the same with the Parmesan cheese. Bake for 45 minutes or until the quiche is set and the crust is browned.

The Conversation

Gathering around a table with friends and family creates intimacy that allows for conversation to flow as easily as coffee from the French press. If your get-together includes people who are new to one another, start the table talk by describing how you and your family know each guest. (And it doesn't have to be Thanksgiving for you to also add why you're grateful for each person present.) Your guests' connection to you becomes a "something in common" foundation that will inspire friendly conversation between mouthfuls of scone and requests to pass the yummy quiche.

The Special Touches

Let's face it. Life is often so busy that when we do finally sit down together with people we enjoy being with, it *is* quite special. With simple and casual touches, from the food choices to the table settings, you can make an indoor gathering memorable.

+ Cut a bunch of pretty flowers or greenery and arrange them in a vase, or use small potted plants such as succulents as a centerpiece.

+ Try placing smaller items atop cake stands or pedestals to give them more height and importance among the dishes.

+ Dim the lights and turn on music for a pleasant mood. Add candles for a cheery glow.

+ Place beverages, scones, and jams on a nearby buffet or console table so guests can choose their favorites before sitting at the table if your dining table is small.

+ Add attractive glass bottles or carafes filled with favorite juices for a vibrant rainbow of beverage options.

THE
Conversation

THE
Conversation

Guests are grateful when they are included in conversations, listened to, and introduced to others. The comfort level and the friendships are what matter most. Small talk can sometimes be awkward, so help engage others in lively conversations. Present an interesting topic to discuss or an intriguing question to start the evening off right, or rally people together with conversation starters during drinks, dinner, or dessert.

We'll look at easy ways to create dining destinations and natural connections between guests, whether they're meeting for the first time or they know one another well. We'll discover simple anyone-and-everyone activities that can shift a gathering from scattered chitchat to group camaraderie before the feast even begins.

Being yourself invites others to be themselves. The moment you relax and let go of any need for perfection, you can focus on your guests, and the discussions and laughter will spark with ease. The heartfelt hospitality you extend from your first *welcome* to your last *thanks for coming* will make each person know their presence mattered.

Being yourself invites others
to be themselves.

33 | INVENT TABLE DESTINATIONS

When you're planning a party—whether it's indoors or outdoors—you can arrange your seating to create conversation hubs and ensure that all of your guests are comfortable conversing and socializing. A few things to consider:

+ Arrange semicircles of chairs, or make sure tables have enough chairs for guests. Keep things flexible so guests can float and mingle.

+ Consider the age of your guests. An old quilt or a blanket on the floor—or a small table—can be a great place for kids to gather. Provide comfortable chairs in easy-to-get-to spaces for older guests.

+ Wander around periodically to make sure everyone is feeling included. Connect guests who have things in common, and make as many introductions as possible.

+ Create cozier conversation hubs for guests who do better in smaller groups. Also, if possible, provide open gathering space for those who like to socialize in a bigger group.

34 | CREATE CONNECTION WITH SEATING

Planning out your seating ahead of time ensures effortless socializing and conversing at your gathering. Take inventory to make sure you have enough seating for all your guests.

Some creative seating ideas might be:

Benches

Ottomans

Big floor pillows

Outdoor furniture brought inside
(or vice versa for an outside party)

Quilts and blankets
(especially for backyard gatherings)

Arrange your furniture and consider a serving style that allows you to get up and move around with ease. That way you can visit with others or help introduce people without having to climb over or under furniture (or other guests).

+ Start with your largest piece, usually your sofa, and add pieces from there.

+ Set furniture close enough together to allow for effortless conversation that won't turn into an unintentional shouting match.

+ Select pieces for seating at similar heights and scale so no one is sitting taller than the others.

+ Place a tray or table within reach of every seat so guests can easily sip a drink and nibble on a treat. Use small stools, stacks of books, or trays on ottomans for surfaces.

+ Make the most of large rooms. Establish more than one conversation area in those spaces. Two chairs in a corner will create a cozy place for a more private conversation.

35 | START THE CONVERSATION

Set out a stack of conversation cards, interesting coffee-table books, or simple group games to serve as activities and conversation starters that offer connection opportunities and put any personality type at ease.

Conversation cards can help connect everyone. Family members or longtime friends who fall into the same old topics will enjoy the interesting or funny lines of dialogue. And guests who don't know one another will appreciate the invitation to be included. If you have guests of varied ages joining you, these cards help bridge the generation gap with conversations that interest everyone.

CONVERSATION STARTERS:

+ If you could choose the free services of a professional for a year, what would you want most: a masseuse, an accountant, a housecleaner, or a chef?

+ When you were young, what did you say you wanted to be when you grew up?

+ If a producer offered to sign you for any past or current reality show, which one would you be on and why?

+ When has a friend or loved one given you a good surprise and what was it? A gift, a compliment, a gathering?

+ If you had to dine on just three foods for the rest of your life, what would you choose?

+ Did you have a favorite birthday party growing up? What was so special about it?

+ What one thing would people be surprised to learn about you?

+ What song would best describe your life?

+ What's your favorite ice cream flavor?

+ If you were stranded on a desert island with just three books, three movies, and three celebrities, what/who would they be?

+ If you started a band, what kind of music would you play? What would your band be called?

36 | LET THE GAMES BEGIN

You can use games at your gathering as a great way to connect. We've had a family tradition for years of playing a wooden board game we call "the marble game." (It's actually called Aggravation.) It's a simple and easy-to-learn game with marbles and dice, but there is little strategy involved. Even young kids can play it. You can select games like this as a "use what you have" centerpiece to serve a dual purpose—an unexpected decoration *and* a way for guests to connect.

+ Set out a checkerboard on an ottoman to encourage interaction with either checkers or chess.

+ Stack a variety of classic family games (Monopoly, Scrabble, Clue, Apples to Apples, Yahtzee, Battleship) on an end table. You can even hand-letter a little sign that encourages guests to feel free to play the games.

+ Set out a basket of simple puzzles, lacing cards, or even plastic horses or dinosaurs for smaller guests to play with.

+ Add a guessing game to the food table. Put jellybeans or M&M's in a mason jar and then ask guests to guess how many candies are in there. Provide small squares of paper and pens so guests can easily write down their guesses. The winner gets to take home the jar of candy!

+ Set aside a few open spaces so guests can sit down with a game. Include enough seating so people can come and go as they please.

🔖 **Simple tip!** Ask your guests to bring their favorite group game.

37 | INTERACT WITH ACTIVITIES

Giving guests something to do is a great way to help start conversations or give people a common ground to engage in conversation. That little bit of inclusion and focus can help ease tension immediately. One terrific idea is a coloring station that will appeal to guests of all ages. It's wonderful to watch various ways people show off their style with their own creative flair and original color schemes. This is super simple, easy, and guaranteed to draw a crowd. You'll need:

+ A selection of coloring books (my *The Inspired Room Coloring Book* is fun *and* decorative!)

+ Containers for the coloring instruments (mason jars, flowerpots, rectangular baskets, and pretty boxes)

+ A selection of crayons, markers, colored pencils, mini pencil sharpeners (with a container to catch pencil shavings), and even watercolor pencils for an outdoor coloring station (add a jar or two of water and fine-tipped paintbrushes)

38 | MAKE SOMETHING TOGETHER

Looking for a goof-proof yet imaginative party activity that combines spending time together with your guests while making a tangible fun memory? These DIY paint pen bottles add a cheerful pop of color to your gathering—and brighten up your guests' homes after the party.

WHAT YOU'LL NEED

Glass bottles, clear or colored
(sparkling clean)

Flowers with long stems
(to fit your glass bottles)

A variety of paint pens
(display several different shades: bright and bold hues, pretty pastels, and glittering metallics)

Directions:

1. **Display** the bottles, pens, and flowers on a designated crafting table.

2. **Pick** a pattern, design, or sweet sentiment to embellish your bottle. Make it easy for your guests by printing out some inspiration such as patterns, quotes, or favorite scriptures.

3. **Share** design idea as you decorate the bottles together.

4. **Add** a coordinating flower to each bottle when you're finished. Oh-so-festive! And as a nice bonus, your gathering now has some personalized decor.

39 | CREATE A PHOTO BOOTH

Photo booths provide a lighthearted, easy party activity and a way for guests to remember the gathering long after everyone has gone home. With just a little preparation, you can create a setting for photo shoots and guest interactions. Get ready to smile!

1. Keep an easy-to-use, digital point-and-shoot camera on hand to snap photos of everyone at a gathering so you can send the photos to them later. Or use an instamatic camera if you have one. Guests can also use their phones to take photos.

2. If you have the extra help, designate someone to be in charge of the photo booth. Ask a few adults or teens to play the role of event photographer.

3. Create a simple backdrop—a colorful sheet or tapestry, a big picture frame, a festive banner.

4. Add accessories and props. Be creative! Gather up feather boas, masquerade masks, leis, Mardi Gras beads, silly glasses, party hats, vintage teacups, crazy scarves, balloons—whatever goes with your theme.

5. Include a mini chalkboard and colored chalk so guests can hand-letter messages and include them in the photo booth fun.

40 | MAP OUT A SCAVENGER HUNT

A scavenger hunt can be a clever theme for a gathering with groups of families. The kids stay moving, and everyone loves the element of adventure. Simply make out a list of creative clues for the kids (and adults!) to follow. This is an activity that a wide range of ages can participate in, and it automatically connects guests. You just need a little bit of advance planning and creativity.

+ Head to your local dollar store for inexpensive prizes. You're sure to find something that matches the theme of your party. (We did a pirate treasure hunt for my son one year and found no shortage of prizes that worked with our limited budget.)

+ For younger kids, keep things simple and hide the clues in plain sight.

+ Think of more complicated clues and hiding places to keep older kids—and adults—busy for a long time. Be creative and make them think!

+ Have your treasure hunters measure distances between items with a measuring tape to help locate a prize, use a compass to find the direction to walk from a landmark, search for clues you set up around the yard, or count steps from a fence or tree to locate the hidden treasures they have to dig up or find in a tree.

+ Plan out a rough estimate of how long the treasure hunt will take. You don't want the treasure to be found in a few minutes, but you also don't want your guests to spend too long trying to find the clues and become frustrated.

41 | DIY: MAKE A TEACUP PLANTER

I'm not a skilled gardener by any stretch of the imagination. I'm quite certain more plants have died in my care than have lived to tell the tale, but I try. I am obsessed with adorable little plants and really do love to take care of them—as long as they live, that is. If you're like me, you'll appreciate this easy craft. (Green thumbs will love it too!) This is a fabulous activity for a wide range of simple gatherings—from garden parties to welcome spring gatherings to any occasion. These little planters look awfully cute on a spring brunch table!

WHAT YOU'LL NEED

Assorted succulents, mosses, or small creeping-type plants

Assorted teacups

Potting soil
(look for special soil for succulents)

Labels and tiny plant stakes to display them

Spray bottle with water

Directions:

1. **Gather** your plants, teacups, and other materials. Lay newspapers on a table (or even place a big tarp on the ground).

2. **Arrange** the above materials, and then let your guests plant and pot and arrange to their heart's content.

3. **Fill** a spray bottle with water so guests can water their new tiny gardens.

🏷 **Simple tip!** Collect old teacups from your own home or scout out thrift shops and discount stores for an inexpensive and creative selection. Chips add character!

LET'S GATHER WITH KIDS
{AN ICE CREAM SUNDAE PARTY}

Now we're ready to take on hosting a gathering for kids! With a little planning, it can be a breeze to host a party that is exciting for children without being overwhelming for the adults. Besides, the delights of childhood are never too far from a mature person's happy place—cheery decorations, engaging activities, special prizes, and tempting treats along with permission to dive right in.

One of my family's favorite ways to gather kids or families together is with an ice cream sundae party. You can create instant conversation with an ice cream station as the main feature or pair this with a BBQ. Either way, it's perfect for both kids and adults alike. Doesn't everyone scream for ice cream?

Granted, a kid-friendly party might not be something you want to sign on for every weekend, but when you think of the many smiles from the day, you'll realize what a gift it is for kids to be kids and for adults to have some kid-like joy.

The Atmosphere

Whether your gathering is *for* kids or intended to be family friendly, always think through what atmosphere and details will work best for the little ones. I think we can safely say, "If the kids are happy, Mom and Dad are happy," (and so are all the guests). Kid-tested party tips will help you create an atmosphere of fun. An added bonus is that these ways to feed and entertain kids are super doable for you.

— ✦ ✦ ✦ —

7 KID-TESTED *PARTY* TIPS

1. Keep plans flexible and organized. Once several kids arrive, the energy rises to surprising levels, and it's easy to lose control if you aren't prepared.

2. Prepare a variety of activities. An outdoor bubble-blowing station, a giant beach ball, or a lawn game will keep your young guests engaged.

3. Consider a shorter guest list when families are invited.

4. Have a kid-proof bedroom ready for naps and a child-friendly DVD on hand in case young guests become restless and adults want to stay longer to talk.

5. Make the party short and sweet. Wind things down before too many meltdowns happen.

6. Round up and purchase a mix of small toys and treats from a discount store. They can be used throughout the evening as silly door prizes or placed in goodie bags at a goodbye station.

7. Purchase spill-proof cups for younger children. It will keep the kiddos dry and lessen Mom and Dad's stress!

The Feast

A simple Sundae Party menu offering lots of topping choices is ideal for kids and all people who like sweet treats. The chocolate-dipped cones are irresistible and provide a homemade touch.

MENU

Ice cream or frozen yogurt

Cones
(sugar, waffle, and/or dipped)

SUGGESTED TOPPINGS

Crumbled candies

Crushed cookies

Fruit

Flavored syrups

Whipped cream

Nuts
(keep separate to be sensitive to those with nut allergies)

Dark chocolate, sea salt, toffee, and coconut for the adventurous

— ✦ ✦ ✦ —

Featured Recipe

CHOCOLATE-DIPPED CONES

Ice cream cones
Sprinkles

Ghiradelli classic white baking chips
(11-ounce bag)

Melt chocolate in a small bowl in the microwave, stirring every 30 seconds or so until smooth. Dip your cones in the bowl of melted chocolate, and then roll them in a small bowl of sprinkles. Prop your cones upright in a cookie cooling rack or the ice cream cone box after cutting small x's to make slots to hold each cone. Allow to cool in the fridge for about 30 minutes.

SUNDAE STATION

To make sure your ice cream station is as adorable as you picture it and simple for your guests to create their ice cream cone masterpieces, plan ahead. Consider where to set it up, which toppings and flavors of ice cream to serve, what utensils guests will need to assemble and eat their sundaes, in what order to bring out the toppings, how to serve the ice cream, and where to seat your guests.

— ✦ ✦ ✦ —

MAKE YOUR SUNDAE STATION A HIT

+ Provide bowls for piling mile-high sundaes, as well as cones for those who love to add a little crunch.

+ If you have a large group, create two stations to help with the traffic flow.

+ Place a stack of baby wipes or damp hand towels nearby to take care of sticky hands and tables.

+ Reduce the table mess by using plastic, oilcloth, easy-to-clean outdoor fabric, or patterned sheets to make simple DIY tablecloths.

+ Designate a helper to assist with spills or refill ice cream as needed.

+ Pre-scoop ice cream into small lidded jars or a single scoop into muffin pans lined with paper cupcake liners and keep frozen in an ice bucket until ready to serve.

The Conversation

Kids—and even some adults—can become distracted when sugar and shiny objects are near! So focus the energy, fun, and conversation with engaging activities. Crafts, games, or creative stations provide children with positive outlets, and they also give parents a way to help or even a chance to take a break when they need it. Most importantly, planned activities playfully encourage guests to interact with one another and create enjoyable memories.

— ✦ ✦ ✦ —

ICE CREAM CREATION CONTEST

Use an instamatic camera, cell phone, or an iPad to capture pictures of each person's ice cream masterpiece. Make the sundae photos a conversation piece by announcing a friendly competition. Invite guests to cast their votes for the most creative, most colorful, most appealing, or most adventurous sundae. Give the winner a grab bag prize or an ice cream scooper as a trophy.

Write the guest's name on the back of the photo, display it on a photo board or a table during the event, and then send the photo home with the guest.

KRAFT PAPER KIDS' TABLE

Provide crayons, markers, and stickers for kids to draw on their own tablecloth. Doing this for the adults' tables as well is a great way to be sure everyone is entertained. Who knows who will want to express their inner artist or break into a game of hangman or tic-tac-toe?

DIY: BUBBLE STATION

It's amazing how bubbles invite kids to be happy and invite adults to be kids, even if just for an afternoon. Plan competitions to see who makes the coolest shapes, the biggest and smallest bubbles, and the most bubbles from one dip of the wand. Here is an easy make-your-own bubble recipe.

WHAT YOU'LL NEED

1 cup light corn syrup

5 cups hot water

1 cup liquid dish soap
(try the blue-colored Dawn)

Bubble wands or pipe cleaners

Lidded glass bottle or container

Directions:

1. **Add** corn syrup to hot water. Whisk until the corn syrup is dissolved.

2. **Add** liquid dish soap slowly and whisk well.

3. **Make** as much mixture as necessary to fill your container.

4. **Let** the solution rest for a few hours before using it.

5. **Buy** bubble wands or bend pipe cleaners into cleverly shaped wands.

Simple tip! Use a large glass beverage dispenser to easily refill paper cups with the bubble solution for the kids.

The Special Touches

Simple ideas will increase the laughter and celebratory experience of your gathering. At the end of the afternoon, as you wipe tiny fingerprints from the sliding glass door and reflect on the kid-friendly gathering, you'll be so glad you decided to create a memorable adventure. I promise.

+ Make the tables vibrant and inviting with patterned napkins, pretty bowls, labels for toppings and drinks, a whimsical garland, confetti, and other unexpected touches.

+ Choose interesting serving pieces, such as cake plates, a tiered serving stand, syrup pourers, and small, colorful bowls for toppings.

+ Get personal when you can! The kids and parents will feel the love when you provide meaningful touches, such as clever name tags, personalized goody bags, individualized beverage labels, or the captioned photos from the ice cream contest.

+ Create and display simple, festive signs out of fabric or paper buntings, chalkboards, or almost anything. For our gathering, we painted an old door with chalkboard paint and wrote a memorable quote on it. These visuals add to the gathering and give you and your guests simple photo opportunities to remember the occasion.

THE
Special
Touches

THE
Special Touches

Intentional details contribute to an unforgettable gathering. Choose a simple but relaxed theme for the food or get-together, prepare a favorite dish, make a homemade dessert or preorder a favorite bakery treat, and arrange a pretty centerpiece. When you include unique extras, your guests will know that you were thinking about them from the very beginning. The special touch is the *personal* touch.

This section will inspire easy additions that make all the difference. If you are at a loss for ideas, take moments to observe the look of your home and your table spread. You'll discover which places need a little TLC and which provide the perfect opportunities to add a generous touch—whether that's a welcome station, a personalized place card, clever labels for drinks, a thoughtful listing of entree ingredients, or takeaway treats such as doggy bags or goody bags.

A gathering doesn't have to be complicated or extravagant to be memorable, but the fruit of your extra effort will show guests that they are thought of and cared about. Your backdrop of special touches won't just transform your home; they'll transform the experience of everyone present—including you!

The special touch is
the personal touch.

42 | SET THE TABLE, SET THE TONE

Start collecting items for your table that can help set the tone for any gathering. A variety of wooden cutting boards can serve both for everyday use and as unique last-minute party platters for cheese, crackers, and bread. Books can elevate plates of cookies and cakes. Small mason jars can be drinking glasses, vases, or containers for candles.

Consider the following to create your own signature presentation:

+ Vary the height of the objects for a more interesting combination of elements.

+ If you are serving meals on your table, make sure your centerpiece is low enough to facilitate easy conversation.

+ Repetition of objects will make a greater impact.

+ Bring out your pretty table linens, place mats, and table runners.

+ Add colorful and patterned dishes that go with the theme of your gathering.

+ Make your own artistic labels for serving dishes or place settings.

43 | SHOWCASE SIMPLE CENTERPIECES

Want to know the secret to a fabulous, no-fuss centerpiece? *Everyday on display.* Chances are you already have a lot of items hiding throughout your house that would be perfect for a centerpiece. Grab a box or basket and start the hunt.

1. **Collect creative containers.** Look for jars, pitchers, bottles, lanterns, vases, trays, platters, bowls, baskets, and crates.

2. **Eye some elevators.** Create interest by arranging items at varying levels using cake plates, books, small wooden boxes, or footed bowls. Gather a variety of candleholders for candles of various sizes.

3. **Gather objects.** Use interesting natural elements to make a statement such as artichokes, pomegranates, pears, seasonal blooms, cornhusks, pumpkins, squashes, and gourds.

4. **Select some fillers.** Once you've chosen a combination of objects that inspire you, decide what fillers you might need to layer in as a base or to finish off the look. Consider eucalyptus branches, moss, small rocks, evergreens, votives, candlesticks, and battery-powered string lights. Place objects and fillers in containers and on elevators.

CREATIVE COMBINATIONS

Hurricane jar + small pebbles + water + floating candle

Stacks of books + teacups + succulent

Glass bowl + water + real or silk flowers

Driftwood wreath + pomegranates + brass candlesticks + white candles

Cloche + ornaments + battery-operated string lights

44 | DIY: CREATE A FABRIC-WRAPPED PLANTER

Fabric-covered pots are a charming addition to any table. Embellish plastic potted plants (or any container) with these easy steps.

WHAT YOU'LL NEED

Small potted plants

Fabric or burlap

Ribbon or twine

Directions:

1. **Measure** the container.

2. **Cut** the fabric or burlap of your choice to fit.

3. **Wrap** fabric around the planters and tuck in the ends.

4. **Tie** ribbon or twine around your pot to secure the ends as needed.

5. **Arrange** as a trio on a tray.

45 | COLLECT VERSATILE ENTERTAINING BASICS

If you don't own a complete set of dishes, don't worry. I don't either! A mix of dishes makes any event informal and imperfect—just right for setting guests at ease.
Some of my favorite table-decorating basics are:

Tiered serving stands

Ceramic or wooden cake plates

Serving bowls and platters

Candles and holders
(various sizes and colors)

Wooden trays or caddies

Glass vases, domes, or hurricanes

Small potted plants or flowers

Natural and seasonal elements
(fruit, pinecones, wreaths, twigs, and moss)

Books for elevating decor
and serving plates

Fabric or ribbon for
wrapping plastic pots

46 | CREATE PRETTY PLACE CARDS

Place cards tell a guest, "You belong. You're important. You have your very own special place at my table." And they're a practical way to add personalized decor to any party. Just use your imagination, think about your theme, and find out-of-the-ordinary ways to welcome your guests to the table.

+ Try pinecones for simple and classic place cards.

+ Write or paint names on colored Easter eggs, and nestle them in a small basket of wheatgrass.

+ Use ribbon to tie a decorative name tag around a pretty napkin.

+ Use baker's twine or jute twine to tie place cards to forks or around flatware.

+ Let the kids make place cards with scrapbooking paper, quirky scissors, colorful pens and pencils, stickers, etc. They will love being involved.

+ Attach festive paper flags with your guests' names to toothpicks, and plant each flag in a small potted succulent or other plant.

+ Tie name tags to soft drink or sparkling juice bottles for each place setting.

47 | LABEL FOOD FOR EFFECT

Party treats are even tastier when you know what you're eating! Eliminate the "what's that dish?" guessing game and tempt your friends to the table with decorative food labels.

+ Use chalkboard labels, wallpaper samples, scrapbooking paper, or an index card folded in half.

+ Cover the buffet or serving table with butcher paper, set down your dishes, and label away to your heart's content. (If you're artistic, you could add delightful little drawings and doodles—or ask a talented family member or friend to lend their talents.)

+ Label foods "Gluten-Free," "Dairy-Free," "Vegan," or "Contains Tree Nuts" to make things easier on your guests with allergies and special dietary needs.

+ Love to play with words? Have fun giving your dishes original titles in keeping with your special theme.

+ The flag-on-a-toothpick labeling method works well on the food table. Have a basket of extra labels on hand for a potluck-style gathering.

48 | ESTABLISH A PARTY DRAWER

Designate a place in your house in which to stash a variety of party supplies. It could be a big drawer, a shelf in the kitchen or pantry, a large storage container in a closet, or anywhere that works in your home. Shopping ahead for items means you'll be ready with very little notice to welcome people into your home.

Some helpful items to keep on hand include:

Mason jars for drinks	A variety of candles *(don't forget birthday candles!)*
Teacups and mugs for hot beverages	Printed paper napkins
Tea bags, powdered hot chocolate and spiced cider packets	Cupcake papers and quick baking mixes
Colorful ribbon	Festive straws

49 | ADD CHARM WITH WASHI TAPE

Washi tape can add pizzazz to so many things—from plastic beverage cups to picture frames to plain jars and containers. These inexpensive rolls of decorative tape (which can be removed from items with ease) come in practically every imaginable color and pattern and make for foolproof craft projects that still look polished and professional. Shop for washi tape that matches the theme or color scheme of your simple gathering and use it to create:

+ Cake flags (with a toothpick)

+ Labels on glasses and serving jars

+ Paper tablecloths

+ Name tags

+ Signs (welcome sign on the front door, sign labeling the guest bathroom)

+ Drink stirrers (with a long toothpick)

+ Cup decorations

+ Twist ties for take-home goody bags

+ Festive garlands

+ Photo borders (perfect for Polaroids!)

+ Cute chopstick designs

LET'S GATHER TO CELEBRATE
{AN AFTERNOON DESSERT}

A great sense of community is formed when a get together is focused on a guest of honor. If you think through your list of friends this very moment, chances are someone in that group is facing a new season, adventure, or milestone. The opportunity to create memories for you, your guests, and the friend being celebrated is an honor. What could be more meaningful than uplifting someone during a significant moment in their life?

A wonderfully simple way to celebrate a special someone is to host an afternoon dessert. A dessert bar with several delicious choices is easy to incorporate into any party. If the gathering overlaps with a typical mealtime, offer a combination of finger foods to go along with the spotlighted sweet offering.

Whether you bring people together for a birthday, engagement, baby shower, or a going-away party, focus on a few special touches and simple activities to show how much you care. This will create a lasting memory for everyone and free you up to be a relaxed and welcoming hostess.

The Atmosphere

Create an atmosphere that will shower the guest of honor with love. What says celebration more than an amazing dessert that caters to your guest of honor's sweet tooth? Find out some of her favorite treats in advance. Think about how celebrated she'll feel when she sees her snack obsessions on the welcome table, her favorite beverages ready to pour, and a spread of her most loved desserts. Does it get any better?

— ✦ ✦ ✦ —

5 DESSERT BAR SUGGESTIONS

These simple tips will help you set up a personalized dessert bar in no time and create an atmosphere that embraces your special guest with friendship and honor.

1. Set up the table in a central location where guests can gather around, take photos, and sample the desserts with ease.

2. Make the dessert bar a decorative focal point for the gathering.

3. Gather a variety of serving dishes, along with small dessert plates, forks, and napkins.

4. Showcase the desserts using pedestals or even stacks of her favorite books or colorful boxes to help elevate them.

5. A dessert bar is the perfect gathering for a potluck!

The Feast

If the requirements for hosting a gathering included cooking and serving a full-course meal, I might panic from all that responsibility and be tempted to call a caterer! If you tend to feel frazzled in the kitchen, why not keep the menu simple and focus most of your attention on making this occasion extra special for the guest of honor? Keep the festivities to drinks and desserts.

MENU

Embellished cakes	Mixed nuts
Saltwater taffy/favorite wrapped candy	Assorted cookies/biscotti
	Punch

EMBELLISHED STORE CAKES

If you love to bake, a dessert bar is your chance to offer some favorite home-made treats. If you don't bake or don't have time, buy a delicious bakery cake and give it your own special touch. There's no shame in that! My daughters and I enjoy decorating simple, tasty cakes with mint leaves, nuts, and fruit. Decorating a bakery cake is easy to do, but it's a little detail that will make your guest of honor feel special.

For an extra-festive look, go a step further and design your own cake flags with patterned washi tape and straws. They are a simple DIY embellishment that can transform any cake to celebration-ready status in a flash. Decorate your cakes just before guests arrive so your embellishments are fresh.

RASPBERRY PUNCH

Sherbet (we use raspberry)
Favorite bubbly drink or lemonade
Mint leaves
Fresh or frozen berries

Moments before your party starts, simply combine the sherbet with your favorite bubbly drink or lemonade. Use mint leaves and berries as a garnish.

The Conversation

These activities and the very easy DIY memory board will connect your guests with one another; provide plenty of opportunities for laughter, stories, and conversations to arise; and center the gathering on the special someone you are all there to honor.

— ✦ ✦ ✦ —

A CARD-MAKING STATION

Provide pretty paper, patterned tape, colored pens, glue sticks, stickers, and other embellishments to add personality so guests can create their own cards for the person of honor. A card-making station provides an immediate way for everyone to show support for the guest of honor, and creativity offers a ready-made way to engage everyone in conversation. The cards can be sent home with the lucky (and loved) guest of honor.

With its assortment of pens and papers, this station effortlessly becomes a pretty gathering space. Make it even more special with balloons, bouquets, or wrapped gifts.

DIY: MAKE A MEMORY BOARD

With one simple DIY project, you can create a conversation piece and even a memento gift for the guest of honor (should you decide to part with it). The memory board becomes a visual reminder of friendship, laughter, and life moments.

WHAT YOU'LL NEED

An old wooden frame
(watch for these at flea markets
and garage sales)

4 Picture wire hooks

1 roll picture wire

1 package of small
clothespins or binder clips

Fabric to fit the frame

Staple gun

Photos of your guest of honor
and/or friends

Directions:

1. **Paint** or whitewash the frame in advance so it has time to dry.

2. **Measure** for even spacing between the wire rows.

3. **Screw** the wire hooks to the underside of the frame.

4. **Cut** 2 lengths of wire a little longer than the width of the frame.

5. **Twist** wire onto the hooks.

6. **Trim** the fabric to fit the frame.

7. **Stretch** the fabric taut and staple it to the back of the frame with the vibrant side facing out.

8. **Clip** photos onto the wires.

Simple tip! Use the finished memory board as part of your gathering's decor or ask guests to bring a photo to add to the board during the event as a collective activity. Either way, something wonderful is created.

The Special Touches

No matter how many times you host a gathering like this, it will feel unique. Why? Because the special touches are based on the guest of honor. Each treat, activity, conversation, and the extras will feel personal and meaningful for that reason. In fact, when the party is over, you just might have a few friends calling to ask if they can be your next guest of honor.

+ Create decorations that honor your special guest.

+ Choose background music your friend will love. Maybe even take a look at her actual playlists a few weeks in advance to get some ideas. Or create a unique soundtrack for the gathering that you can then gift to the guests.

+ If your special guest won't mind the attention, decorate a guest-of-honor chair or surround it with bouquets of her favorite flowers.

+ Invite those who gather to shower the guest of honor with sentiments of friendship, a special memory, or a word of appreciation.

+ Present parting gifts that represent the guest of honor. Fill decorative bags with her favorite candy or other sweet treat.

Conclusion

50 | DREAM OF YOUR NEXT SIMPLE GATHERING

As I confessed earlier, I was only able to follow my desire to share my home because I recognized my weaknesses and focused on my strengths. I hope this look at simple gatherings has helped you identify the areas of hosting that are the most difficult for you and those that are the most enjoyable and well-suited to your personality and style.

So...what *will* you plan now?

Do you have visions of your next simple gathering dancing in your head? Take time to go back over your favorite tips and lists in this book and let your ideas flow. Be encouraged to create your own wonderful get-together.

Whatever you do, I know it will be great. And as soon as you wave goodbye to a guest who is grinning ear to ear, you can be sure that you'll want to plan another gathering that is as enjoyable and intentional. You have what it takes to make each gathering a treasured experience for you and your guests.

— ✦ ✦ ✦ —

The deepest joy in life is found
when we simply gather.

MAKE YOUR HOME A SANCTUARY—NOT A SHOWPLACE

Welcome to *The Inspired Room*. Forget about the rules and discover inspired ways to personalize your spaces and express your style with texture, color, and your favorite treasures. Room by room, you'll shape a home that is inspired by the people, beauty, and life you love.

Step inside Melissa's home as she shares lessons learned, inspiring photos, and encouraging insights to help you embrace your authentic style.

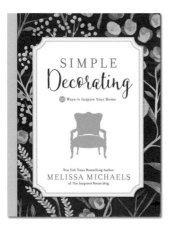

CREATE A HOME YOU CAN'T WAIT TO COME HOME TO

Jump-start your style and refresh your home with this gathering of budget-friendly and practical ideas to help you get unstuck, reimagine your spaces, and transform hard-to-love areas into favorite destinations.

With more than 300 tips to motivate you along the way, this is the perfect guide to break you out of your decorating rut and get you excited about your home again. Let Melissa show you how easy it is to make small changes with big results.

TAKE BACK YOUR SPACE AND LOVE YOUR HOME AGAIN

CREATE THE HOME OF YOUR DREAMS RIGHT WHERE YOU ARE

You can love your home again. Join Melissa as she helps you look past the tiny flaws, every-day messes, and the mix of hand-me-down furniture and focus on what truly matters— how your home shapes your life, relationships, and dreams.

Dare to see your surroundings with new eyes that just might inspire a change of heart. And get ready to *Love the Home You Have.*

CLEAR OUT THE CLUTTER AND MAKE ROOM FOR WHAT MATTERS

If all the stuff you have is starting to take over your home and life, let Melissa offer insightful ideas for altering your habits while efficiently decluttering and organizing you home so you can really enjoy living there.

With a little encouragement and practical advice, you will be inspired to create a place for the things you love and breathing room to pursue your dreams and engage in life with the people who matter most.

ABOUT THE
Author

MELISSA MICHAELS is the creator and author of the popular home decorating blog *The Inspired Room*, which inspires women to love the home they have. Since 2007 Melissa has been encouraging hundreds of thousands of readers a month with daily posts and inspiration for all things house and home. *The Inspired Room* was twice voted as the *Better Homes and Gardens* magazine Reader's Choice decorating blog.

Melissa lives with her husband, Jerry; their son, Luke; and two impossibly adorable Doodle pups, Jack and Lily, whose adventures are well loved and followed on their Facebook page (Facebook.com/jack.goldendoodle). The Michaels' daughters, Courtney and Kylee (and Kylee's husband, Lance), are an active part of *The Inspired Room*.

CONNECT WITH MELISSA AND OTHER HOME LOVERS

The Inspired Room Blog — **theinspiredroom.net**

Subscribe — Have new blog posts delivered to your inbox.

melissa@theinspiredroom.com.

Facebook.com/**theinspiredroom.fans**

Instagram
Pinterest — **@theinspiredroom**
Twitter